BECOMING
ESQUIRE

BECOMING ESQUIRE

"THIS BOOK IS FOR YOUR 3 A. M. BRAIN"

A Law School
Survival Guide Series

CARLETTA SANDERS

BECOMING ESQUIRE:
A Law School Survival Guide Series

Copyright © 2020 by Carletta Sanders

All Rights Reserved

PRINTED IN THE UNITED STATES OF AMERICA

Published by Carletta Sanders
Edited By: Meredith Stange

ISBN 978-0-578-72838-4

Book Cover Design Sophisticated Press LLC

The Juris Society™ is registered
with the U.S Patent and Trademark Office and
therefore may not be duplicated.

Table of Contents

Acknowledgements viii

Chapter 1: Why Law School? 1

Chapter 2: Before you Begin LSAT Prep 9

Chapter 3: It's On: LSAT Prep Begins 17

Chapter 4: Everyone Isn't Harvard Bound .. 56

Chapter 5: Finding Your Tribe 70

A Note About The Author 81

Acknowledgements

I dedicate this book to my late grandfather, Reverend Allen Dennis. He was the very first person that I told that I wanted to be a lawyer at a very young age. He told me that I could be anything that I wanted to be in this world. I was crazy enough to believe him and here we are today. Although my grandfather is no longer with us physically, I know that he's got the best seat in the house and cheering me on proudly throughout this process. The person that I am is because of the lessons that he instilled in me during the time that he graced this earth. I will take them with me to the end of time.

Thank you to my law school family. To my professor Meredith Stange for believing in my vision for this book and allowing me to share her 3 a.m. Brain concept. Additionally, for assisting me along the way with sound advice, edits, and overall dedication to this book. To my Law Professor Theresa Clarke for providing feedback on citing.

Finally, to my tribe (this includes you) for being my biggest supporters on my journey to law. I am forever grateful for all of your prayers, encouragement, and contributions.

CHAPTER 1

Why Law School?

You hear it all of the time: law school is a road less traveled and it is even more less traveled for minorities. You've heard of the scary LSAT and the preparation it will take to perform well. You've heard of intense law school stories and 90% of you have seen "The Paper Chase" and "Legally Blonde" and yet you are here. Some of you are the first-generation graduates and law students, others of you may come from a long lineage of lawyers and judges. Some of you started in low-income housing or middle-class families and other students upper class. Regardless of your upbringing and education, each of you has a story to tell, something or someone that motivated you on this journey to Esquire.

I challenge you to "focus on your why". You will see this concept throughout this chapter and others as a reminder when you are feeling overwhelmed and that no one understands the amount of stress you are going through. Remain focused. Remaining focused will assist in eliminating self-doubt. In fact, you will be so focused on attaining your goal of getting into law school that any thoughts of "what if" or "I can't" will be pushed out of your mind. Your "why's" will outweigh a rough study day or a disappointing test score. Focus gives you the push you need to get through one more set of logic games before bed and getting up the next morning and doing it all over again. Remaining focused and true to the various reasons why you started this journey will guide you through.

There are three questions that I beseech you to ponder on throughout this chapter. First being: **Why do you want to be an attorney?** You will get this question quite often once you begin to express your interest in law to others. I would suggest answering this question for yourself through honest self-reflection. For some it will be to make money, have status , put the "bad guys" in prison, using the degree to help shape laws , protect the innocent, help disadvantaged and impoverished citizens, or simply following in the footsteps before you. What is YOUR reason? Understand that it may not be a canned answer that your reasoning may be singular to you and your life experiences. Whatever it may be, use it as fuel throughout this journey.

Similar to the last question, the next question is: **Why is the goal of "becoming Esquire" important to you?** In the United States, in order to become a licensed attorney (Esquire) you must take and pass a bar examination in order to be admitted to the bar and practice law in that particular jurisdiction. With that, you are legally allowed to practice in that state. Why is that important to you? For some, it will be because they want to start their own firm or work at their parent's firm. Others, to become an associate at a firm, a government agency or nonprofit, to become a public defender or a prosecutor or simply use their juris doctor as the means to professionally advance where you are currently employed.

Lastly, **how will this degree and license impact your life as well as others?** This coincides with the previous questions but pushes you to dig deeper. For some, it's not just about you. It's about making your family proud, making sure that your grandparents are taken care of, or providing for your partner and children. Additionally, it may also be about providing services to your own community, or any community for that matter. It may be about being able to serve your clients with the needed confidence such as assisting business owners by drafting theirs contracts or filing federal trademarks, representing an unprotected battered spouse, and requesting a protective order, or being in court for criminal cases. Understanding that you will become part of a career that can directly affect someone's freedom, or someone's livelihood allows you to acknowledge and consider the seriousness and importance of the "why".

3 a.m. Brain

My Legal Writing professor, Professor Stange, introduced me to the concept of the 3 a.m. brain. She told us that the 3 a.m. brain is what makes us wake up at 3 a.m. and be suddenly panicked about something minor that we are convinced is of the utmost importance. Then we usually wake up later and wonder why we were so worried. We've all had instances where our "3 a.m. brain" has gotten the best of us. You know, it's the reason you put 2+ 2 in a calculator or reread questions on an exam for several minutes even though you've already grasped the gist on the first read. It's what makes you think that you've missed a deadline that you've written down numerous times and have properly prepared for. It's what wakes you up in the middle of the night (if you have the privilege of getting a good night's rest) fearing that you've totally failed an exam for misspelling the professor's name or not adding the required foot note. Your 3 a.m. brain leaves you panicked in instances where ultimately nothing is wrong.

My 3 a.m. brain caused me to send an email to my professor in the wee hours of the morning to discuss a potential plaintiff for battery on the Doctrine of Transfer intent. This email seemed to go on forever, frantic in structure, until I felt that I had gotten my point across and justified my reasoning. After sending it, I felt that I could not rest until she read the email and gave me feedback.

I finally received a response and guess what? I was wrong. She went on to give advice that I will now extend to you: It is always good to go back and rethink issues but don't spend too much time because it will make you worry about things that you can't change. Why is this important? Your 3 a.m. brain will make you second guess the information that you've studied. At times, it will make you rethink your entire decision of law school BUT don't let it. This is why remaining focused is vital. Know that it will happen. You get to "freak out" through this process. You get to take a break and relieve stress but always keep your end goal with you.

Of course, your 3 a.m. brain will cause you to think things that may not be entirely true and here is where refocusing your thoughts and energy will benefit you most. Remember WHY you want to achieve your goals. Don't let it overcome you and stop you from taking a step that will get you closer to attaining your lawyer goals. Becoming more organized and creating a schedule will be beneficial to maximizing your time but it can also be used to combat your 3 a.m. brain. While this journey can and is for many of us taxing, tenacity and resiliency will serve you well.

The LSAT (Law School Admission Test) is supposed to give everyone a fair playing field. There are no advantages here. There is no elevator, in fact everyone takes the "stairs" in this instance. While some may be better test takers, this Exam tests learnable concepts. You get to decide how you choose to study and how much time you want to put into studying. There are sacrifices that will be made throughout this journey and there will be times that you want to quit. In those moments, refer back to the three questions asked previously.

1. Why do you want to be an attorney?

2. Why is the goal of "becoming Esquire" important to you?

3. How will this degree and license impact your life as well as others?

Use it as motivation. Write your answers down because it makes your goals more tangible and real. You can see it, feel it, and it's no longer a concept.

Understand that for most of you, this will be the most challenging and laborious journey (both academically and personally) that you will encounter thus far. Remaining focused allows you to weather the "storm" and take each portion of this journey in strides. You get to rest but you don't get to quit. Let's get started.

CHAPTER 2

Before you Begin LSAT Prep

It is important to note that LSAT prep can be costly. Adequately preparing for such prep will not only save you money but also time. There are four steps that can assist in "pre-prep" for the LSAT before you begin studying.

1. Understanding the LSAT and its components:

The Law School Admission Test (LSAT) has 4 sections.

a) Reading Comprehension

b) Analytical Reasoning (or Logic games)

c) Logic Reasoning

d) Writing Sample

Each section is 35 minutes and all sections are multiple choice, exempting the writing sample, which is always last. The LSAT is given in six separate parts (five scored and one unscored). There are two scored Logic Reasoning (LR) testing sections, one scored Reading Comprehension(RC) section, one scored Analytical Reasoning (known as Logic Games) section, one scored Writing Sample and lastly one unscored section that could be any of the three multiple choice sections mentioned above.

You won't know which section is unscored and this unscored section is utilized as a group of possible questions for future tests.

On the LSAT, you only get points for the questions that you answer correctly. PLEASE DO NOT LEAVE ANY QUESTIONS BLANK and go with your best guess. Determine what answer choice you will utilize for questions that you're not sure about. An example strategy of this would be sticking with one answer choice for those particular questions that you either didn't get to or questions that you are unsure about instead of blindly choosing a different answer choice each time. (i.e. choosing answer choice "c")

2. Creating a Law School Admission Counsel (LSAC) account.

LSAC.org is a centralized location that stores all LSAT scores, letters of recommendations, official transcripts, and law school applications. Your LSAC account will be needed to view and register for LSAT dates. Additionally, LSAC has LSAT prep (Khan Academy) and also have registration for law school forums that are held nationwide in which perspective law students can meet with different law schools to discuss admissions related topics.

3. Determine your avenue(s) of studying AND financial means to pay for them.

Now that you understand the LSAT and its components, you can determine how you will study for it. There is no "right" way to study for the LSAT. Different methods can garner the same results for test takers. There are numerous ways to prepare for the

LSAT and the price can range from free to thousands of dollars. The list below are different avenues in which most test takers prepare for the LSAT.

- Online course OR in-class course (i.e. Kaplan LSAT, Princeton Law Review, 7Sage)
- Self-Study with FREE Material and/or LSAT Prep Books (i.e. The Official LSAT Prep PLUS via Law School Admission Council (LSAC), Power Score Bibles and the LSAT Trainer)
- One-on-One personal tutor (varies)
- A mixture thereof

The examples listed above are the most well-known means of LSAT prep however it is not a fully exhausted list of LSAT resources. They are a good place to start foundationally if you have not yet determined your mode of prep.

4. Determining your "Game Plan"

First things first, determine which LSAT test date you will register for.

The LSAT is offered eight or nine times a year on average. Most college students opt to take the LSAT in the summer (June or July) because it allows more time for studying due to summer break. However, there are additional later test dates throughout the year to choose which will work the best based on your circumstances.

Second, take a blind LSAT (where there is no preparation.) This blind test can be timed or untimed, but it is best to take exams under the conditions in which they will be given for the most accurate score. You can take an LSAT from the LSAC website. There are free LSATS online that have answer keys.

This is the best way to understand where you are starting and what you need to focus on.

Make note of every questions that you took a guess on. This will again, assist in determining what you actually know. The goal here is not to create false hope in which you believe that you know more about topics when you actually do not. This makes you less likely to adequately focus on the topic itself. Also, if you receive a score that you are not happy with, do not be discouraged. For many, the concepts on the LSAT are extremely foreign. I urge you to see it as an opportunity for growth because that's exactly what it is. Regardless of what you score, review the answer key and explanations.

Lastly, determine how many hours per day/ week will be dedicated to preparing for the LSAT (based on your blind LSAT score and the number of points you want to increase your score by.)

Set realistic goals in both: your target LSAT score and plan of attack.

Be realistic is planning. Only you know your discipline. The goal is NOT to overexert, and cause burn out before the exam. The goal instead is to maximize the time you allot. At this point, many decide on a "target score" because it allows you to track your progress throughout the process. While others will aim for "as high as they can get". Determine which approach works best for you. Factors to take into consideration: The date that you will take the LSAT: Again, typically summer testing allots for more time due to summer break for students. If the test date is later in the year, proper planning around school scheduling will be needed. You have to decide how much time will be needed to get to where you want to be. Be realistic in this goal setting. On average the rule of thumb is 3 months for LSAT prep but can and will be longer for some depending on their methods of studying and time allotted based on each individual.

Whether or not you will be working during prep: Everyone does not have the luxury of studying for the LSAT full time for personal reasons. I would advise that if you have to work, to at least reduce hours where and if possible. Additionally, utilize any downtime at your job to study which includes breaks and coming in early and/or staying late to ensure that you have reached your goal for the day.

As it pertains to determining study plans, keep in mind that you all grasps concepts differently. For some test takers, three hours daily study time will suffice while it may take additional hours for others. Moreover, early morning studying may not be beneficial for all but instead late-night studying or fragmented studying throughout the day. Study plans are singular to you and therefore should be personalized.

Lastly, understand that your study plan is not concrete, and it may be necessary to tweak it to better fit your personal needs. However, simply choosing not to study because you "don't feel like it" or making excuses to not study only hurts yourself. This is where focusing on your Chapter questions 1 will benefit you.

Please be fully aware that the LSAT will push you to fullest and it is necessary pressure. Treat the LSAT as you would a new job. This advice will continue to serve you well throughout law school. How much time and effort are you willing to put in to exceling at your new job?

CHAPTER 3

It's On: LSAT Prep Begins

The LSAT is your new job and today is your first day. You want to make a good impression so you've prepared as much as you can; you have your game plan and your blind LSAT score.

At this point, it's time to focus on learning and conceptualizing the topics in each section. Start with whichever section you would like. Before starting breakdown of each section, below is one tip that will assist with the LSAT as a whole and is not section specific.

Practice time management. Some students fail to get to the last questions or passages due to poor time management. Starting timed sections earlier rather than later will assist in getting faster at answering questions.

You will get faster eventually through practice because you in learning how to manage your time properly. This is trial and error but trying earlier in your prep will allow for adjustments in sections. Additionally, determining your strategy for individual sections will also assist in passage completion. It's important to note that your time spent on each section will decrease as you develop a strategy for answering the questions. Developing this strategy may take some time so don't be upset if it takes you longer in your beginning stage of studying. This is why continued practice will help you better manage your time as your prep continues.

The Reading Comprehension(RC) Section has 3 main portions: The Question Stem, which is the actual question (i.e. Which answer reflects the main point of the passage above?), Next is the Stimulus(passage), which is the argument or set of facts to read, and lastly the Answer Choices themselves.

Reading Comprehension Section:

Reading Comprehension (RC) section typically contains 27 questions and 3 individual passages and 1 paired passage (2 passages for a set of questions).Ideally, you should spend around 8-9 minutes per passage.

Below are three tips that can be implemented to assist with the Reading Comprehension (RC) section.

1. Determine the order of passages: Before beginning the RC section, briefly scan and number the passages in the order that you will complete them. The most common way to order your passages is from easiest to hardest based on keywords & structure. Even consider the tone of the author. Some students will opt to start with a shorter passage first or passages that have terms that are easier to understand. Others will determine the question order by looking at the answer choices to make a quick guess about what needs to be determined to answer the questions.

More specific to structure, be sure to circle key terms such as "like, but, however, although". These are transitional words and can assist in questions asking about the author's feelings toward the subject in the passage.

Typically, the RC paired passage is used for comparative reading in which the topic is common, but the passages have similarities and differences. Questions that could be presented include comparing the different approaches to a certain fact in the passages. More often than not, the prompt will give clues on where to look for this information.

Do not make the mistake of choosing the order based on subject matter, for example, politics or literature. Making this mistake can result in you spending more time on a more complex passage and possibly leaving points on the table by not leaving enough time for passages that were easier to complete.

2. Understand the question stem: This tip requires you to read the question stem in a way that you can reflect on "What is this question stem asking me?" This will assist in identifying the question type (i.e. main point question stem which asks for the overall conclusion of the passage).

Other question stems include the purpose of the passage, main point (as stated above), structure etc.

Questions that could come from the stems include:

a) What is the purpose of this passage?

b) How does the author view [x's] ….?

With that, you can decide based off of the information above, which passages you want to tackle in a particular order.

For some, the paired passage maybe easier while others may decide to take on the passages based on the keywords themselves.

Nonetheless, you shouldn't be afraid to try different orders during the practice tests to maximize your score.

3. Read the passages strategically: RC differs greatly from leisure reading so don't fall into the trap of being too relaxed. You want to actively read the passage, including circling key words and using your margins as a place to take notes and roadmap passages to identify the most important points and be better able to summarize the passages. This will assist in predicting where the passage is going in order to better answer the questions.

Practicing this active reading will allow you to save time so that you won't have to waste time rereading passages.

Overall, with this section, have a goal in mind as to how many passages you want to get to and work towards that goal. Make note that it is possible that you may not get to all of the passages completely but getting as close as possible will contribute to your increasing your overall score. Work hard on the sections that you can get to. For the remaining: scan and make your best guess. Again, leave nothing blank.

Reading Comprehension Sample Question: [1]

Directions: Each set of questions in this section is based on a single passage or a pair of passages. The questions are to be answered on the basis of what is **stated** or **implied** in the passage or pair of passages. For some questions, more than one of the choices could conceivably answer the question. However, you are to choose the **best answer;** that is, choose the response that most accurately and completely answers the question.

Stimulus or Passage:

The painter Roy Lichtenstein helped to define pop art—the movement that incorporated commonplace objects and commercial-art techniques into paintings—by paraphrasing the style of comic books in his work. His merger of a popular genre with the forms and

---

[1] Law School Admissions Council, Reading Comprehension Sample Questions, https://www.lsac.org/lsat/taking-lsat/test-format/reading-comprehension/reading-comprehension-sample-questions (last visited July 2, 2020).

intentions of fine art generated a complex result: while poking fun at the pretensions of the art world, Lichtenstein's work also creatively managed to convey a seriousness of theme that enabled it to transcend mere parody.

That Lichtenstein's images were fine art was at first difficult to see, because, with their word balloons and highly stylized figures, they looked like nothing more than the comic book panels from which they were copied. Standard art history holds that pop art emerged as an impersonal alternative to the histrionics of abstract expressionism, a movement in which painters conveyed their private attitudes and emotions using nonrepresentational techniques. The truth is that by the time pop art first appeared in the early 1960s, abstract expressionism had already lost much of its force. Pop art painters weren't quarreling with the powerful early abstract expressionist work of the late 1940s but with a second generation of abstract expressionists whose work seemed airy, high-minded, and overly lyrical. Pop art paintings were full of simple black lines and large areas of primary color. Lichtenstein's work was part of a general rebellion against the fading emotional power of abstract expressionism, rather than an aloof attempt to ignore it.

But if rebellion against previous art by means of the careful imitation of a popular genre were all that characterized Lichtenstein's work, it would possess only the reflective power that parodies have in relation to their subjects. Beneath its cartoonish methods, his work displayed an impulse toward realism, an urge to say that what was missing from contemporary painting was the depiction of contemporary life. The stilted romances and war stories portrayed in the comic books on which he based his canvases, the stylized automobiles, hot dogs, and table lamps that appeared in his pictures, were reflections of the culture Lichtenstein inhabited. But, in contrast to some pop art, Lichtenstein's work exuded not a jaded cynicism about consumer culture, but a kind of deliberate naiveté, intended as a response to the excess of sophistication he observed not only in the later abstract expressionists but in some other pop artists. With the comics—typically the domain of youth and innocence—as his reference point, a nostalgia fills his paintings that gives them, for all their surface bravado, an inner sweetness. His persistent use of comic-art conventions clearly demonstrates a faith in reconciliation, not only between cartoons and fine art, but between parody and true feeling.

Question Stem (the actual question):

Question 1. Which one of the following best captures the author's attitude toward Lichtenstein's work?

Answer Choices:

a) enthusiasm for its more rebellious aspects

b) respect for its successful parody of youth and innocence

c) pleasure in its blatant rejection of the abstract expressionism

d) admiration for its subtle critique of contemporary culture

e) appreciation for its ability to incorporate both realism and naivete

Below are the correct answers and explanations.

This question requires the test taker to understand the author's attitude toward Lichtenstein's work.

The correct response is (E). Response (E) most accurately and completely captures the author's attitude. The author's appreciation for Lichtenstein's art is indicated by way of contrast with the way in which the author describes what Lichtenstein's art is not. For example, the author asserts that Lichtenstein's work "transcended mere parody," and that unlike other pop art, it did not display a "jaded cynicism." Similarly, the author holds that there is more to Lichtenstein's work than "the reflective power that parodies possess in relation to their subjects." Moreover, the author's appreciation is reflected in several positive statements of Lichtenstein's work. The author's appreciation for Lichtenstein's realism is indicated by the author's statement that "Beneath its cartoonish methods, his work displayed an impulse toward realism, also an urge to say that what was missing from contemporary painting was the depiction of contemporary life." That the author also appreciates Lichtenstein's naiveté is demonstrated in this sentence: "Lichtenstein's work exuded not a jaded cynicism about consumer culture, but a kind of deliberate naiveté..." This idea is further expanded in the next sentence, which says that "for all their surface bravado," Lichtenstein's paintings possess "an inner sweetness." It is important to note that these evaluations appear in the last paragraph and form part of the author's conclusion about the importance of Lichtenstein's art.

Response (A) is incorrect because, although in the last sentence of paragraph two the author notes Lichtenstein's connection to a general rebellion against abstract expressionism, the author also states quite pointedly in the first sentence of the third paragraph:

"But if rebellion ... were all that characterized Lichtenstein's work, it would possess only the reflective power that parodies have..."

Response (B) is incorrect because, as noted in the first paragraph of the passage, the author believes Lichtenstein's work transcended "mere parody." Moreover, the author states in the last paragraph that comics, "typically the domain of youth and innocence," were Lichtenstein's "reference point" and filled his painting with "nostalgia" and an "inner sweetness."

Response (C) is incorrect because, as mentioned above, the author believes Lichtenstein's rebellion against abstract expressionism was not the most important aspect of his work. Indeed, if it had been, Lichtenstein's work would have been reduced to having "only the reflective power that parodies have in relation to their subjects," where here the "subject" refers to abstract expressionism.

Response (D) is incorrect because the author very clearly says that Lichtenstein embraced contemporary culture. In the last paragraph, the author writes, "But, in contrast to some pop art, Lichtenstein's work exuded not a jaded cynicism about consumer culture, but a kind of deliberate naiveté..."

Analytical Reasoning (or Logic Games) Section:

Many students find difficulty in this section and I would suggest approaching this section with the mindset that the LSAT has learnable concepts and each section can be mastered with consistence. The best tips for this section is understanding the types of Logic games and its strategies and practice questions.

Logic Games section consists of four games with 5-7 questions per section (23 questions total) This gives approximately 8-9 minutes per game for timing.

The components of Analytical Reasoning (or Logic Games) include:

a) a section that gives you a task

b) a section that gives you the rules needed to complete the task

c) Questions & answer choices

There are three most common types of games that you will encounter in this section:

a. **Matching Games**: consists of two or more categories that you have to match together but they do not have to be in a particular order

b. **Sequencing Games**: the most common type and it requires you to place things or selections in a specific order.

These questions primarily involve one specific set of variables and a separate set of spaces for the order to be answered.

Criteria typically includes:

> **Numbers**
>
> **Days of the week**

Classroom/ movie theater seating

These types of games are easily identifiable because you will be able to see that there is 1 variable per space. An example of this would be 3 students watching movies on 3 separate days of the week.

c. **Grouping Games**: This type of games closely resemble sequencing except that there is no 1:1 ratio for variable and spaces. Here, variables can be placed in many different categories.

Ex. being a part of a team and wearing a full colored or patterned shirt. Additionally, there is another type called Hybrid games that you can encounter in which the game is a combination of the types.

Formal Logic:

It appears in most if not all of the logic games as "if/then". This will come in different forms such as: if/then/ if only, unless, if and only if.

Taking the time to properly understand the different forms will be extremely beneficial to mastering Logic Games.

The following execution tips will be beneficial to utilize in mastering Logic Games.

1. Complete the easy questions first

2. Be sure to read and review everything (including the questions!)

3. Accurately write out the rules (could be listed as conditions) & draw inferences to help create a master rule.

4. Complete the hardest questions last & if you're stuck, move on.

Analytical Reasoning (Logic Games) Sample Question: [2]

---

[2] Law School Admissions Council, Analytical Reason Sample Questions, https://www.lsac.org/lsat/taking-lsat/test-format/analytical-reasoning/analytical-reasoning-sample-questions (last visited July 2, 2020).

Directions:

Each set of questions in this section is based on a scenario with a set of conditions. The questions are to be answered on the basis of what can be **logically inferred** from the scenario and conditions. For each question, choose the response that **most accurately** and completely answers the question.

Passage for Question 1

A university library budget committee must reduce exactly five of eight areas of expenditure—G, L, M, N, P, R, S, and W—in accordance with the following conditions:

1. If both G and S are reduced, W is also reduced.

2. If N is reduced, neither R nor S is reduced.

3. If P is reduced, L is not reduced.

4. Of the three areas L, M, and R, exactly two are reduced.

Question 1

If both M and R are reduced, which one of the following is a pair of areas neither of which could be reduced?

a. G, L

b. G, N

c. L, N

d. L, P

e. P, S

Below is the correct answer and explanations.

Explanation for Question 1

This question concerns a committee's decision about which five of eight areas of expenditure to reduce. The question requires you to suppose that M and R are among the areas that are to be reduced, and then to determine which pair of areas could not also be among the five areas that are reduced.

The fourth condition given in the passage on which this question is based requires that exactly two of M, R, and L are reduced. Since the question asks us to suppose that both M and R are reduced, we know that L must not be reduced:

Reduced: M, R

Not reduced: L

The second condition requires that if N is reduced, neither R nor S is reduced. So N and R cannot both be reduced. Here, since R is reduced, we know that N cannot be. Thus, adding this to what we've determined so far, we know that L and N are a pair of areas that cannot both be reduced if both M and R are reduced:

Reduced: M, R

Not reduced: L, N

Answer choice (C) is therefore the correct answer, and you are done.

When you are taking the test, if you have determined the correct answer, there is no need to rule out the other answer choices. However, for our purposes in this section, it might be instructive to go over the incorrect answer choices. For this question, each of the incorrect answer choices can be ruled out by finding a possible outcome in which at least one of the two areas listed in that answer choice are reduced. Consider answer choice (A), which lists the pair G and L. We already know that for this question L must be one of the areas that is not reduced, so all we need to consider is whether G can be one of the areas that is reduced. Here's one such possible outcome:

Reduced: M, R, G, S, W

If areas M, R, G, S, and W are reduced, then the supposition for the question holds and all of the conditions in the passage are met:

> M and R are both reduced, as supposed for this question.

Both G and S are reduced, and W is also reduced, so the first condition is satisfied.

N is not reduced, so the second condition is not relevant.

P is not reduced, so the third condition is not relevant.

Exactly two of L, M, and R are reduced, so the fourth condition is satisfied.

Thus, since G could be reduced without violating the conditions, answer choice (A) can be ruled out. Furthermore, since G appears in the pair listed in answer choice (B), we can also see that (B) is incorrect.

Now let's consider answer choice (D), which lists the pair L and P. We already know that for this question L must be one of the areas that is not reduced, so all we need to consider is whether P can be one of the areas that is reduced. Here's one such possible outcome:

Reduced: M, R, P, S, W

If areas M, R, P, S, and W are reduced, then the supposition for the question holds and all of the conditions in the passage are met:

M and R are both reduced, as supposed for this question.

> G is not reduced, so the first condition is not relevant.
>
> N is not reduced, so the second condition is not relevant.
>
> P is reduced and L is not reduced, so the third condition is satisfied.

Exactly two of L, M, and R are reduced, so the fourth condition is satisfied.

Since P could simply be reduced without violating the conditions, answer choice (D) can be ruled out.

Furthermore, since P appears in the pair listed in answer choice (E), we can also see that answer choice (E) is incorrect.

The most commonly selected incorrect answer choice was response (E).

Logic Reasoning Sections:

Logic Reasoning has 2 scored sections on a traditional LSAT. With that, these sections are worth nearly 50% of your score. Each section has 24-26 questions. You have approximately 1 minute and 25 sec (more or less) to answer each question and bubble in. It goes without saying (but I will anyway) mastering these sections are vital to your LSAT success and even as a law student.

In these sections, you will have to read short passages and answer questions about each such as identifying the flaw in an argument.

The overall purpose is to get you to analyze and examine arguments in passages. This is where drawing conclusions, identifying assumptions made by the argument and being able to properly analogize by reasoning.

Like, Logic Games, this section has different questions types. They are as followed: [3]

a) **Flaw Questions** ask you to spot the underlying flaw in each of the arguments presented.

b) **Assumption Questions** ask you to identify the gap between the evidence provided and the conclusion reached. The right answer choice will be the statement that is necessary to get from the evidence to the conclusion.

c) **Inference Questions** ask to find the statement that is most supported by the argument, assuming all the statements in the argument are accurate.

---

[3] Allyson Evans, Top Tips For LSAT Logical Reasoning. Magoosh LSAT Blog (April 19, 2019).

d) **Strengthen Questions** ask you to recognize the statement that would best bolster the author's argument and support the conclusion.

e) **Weaken Questions** ask you to spot the statement that would most detract from the author's evidence in support of the conclusion.

f) **Paradox Questions** ask you to note the answer choice with the most similar argument structure to the one in the argument.

g) **Principle Questions** ask you to choose the answer choice that is an example of the idea, or principle, presented in the argument.

Tips to assist in this sections are below.

1. Know the question type: This will allow you to at least start with the proper foundation to answering the questions correctly because each question type has different "rules" to answer them. Therefore, having a clear understanding of each type will benefit you here.

2. Actively reach the question and the evaluate answer choices. Be sure to practice ACTIVE READING here. Just as we discussed in Reading Comp. section, road mapping is key. Actively reading also include quickly reviewing the question type to be sure that you are staying on track. Always ask yourself "What is the question asking me to do?"

Evaluating the answer choices are key as well because you don't want to get the question wrong because you didn't take the time to review and examine the choices. Traditionally, there are answer choices that are just flat out wrong. Here is where you eliminate them and move on. Also, there's typically 2 answer choices that seem to both be correct. Analyzing these two choices carefully can make the difference. Often times it is slight differences in wording that can change the answer choice completely. Pay attention to this.

3. Move On! Don't waste too much time on questions if you are having difficulty getting through it. Circle it (give your best guess) and move on. Remember, you get

scored by the number of questions that you get correct! In order to maximize your score, you have to at least get to the questions.

Completing practice exams is exactly where this can be improved. You get to go back and determine why you were having such difficulty and REVIEW the section pertaining to it. Better to do that , than to not have this opportunity on the actual exam.

Logic Reasoning Sample Question:[4]

Executive: We recently ran a set of advertisements in the print version of a travel magazine and on that magazine's website. We were unable to get any direct information about consumer response to the print ads. However, we found that consumer response to the ads on the website was much more limited than is typical

---

[4] Law School Admissions Council, Logical Reasoning Sample Questions, https://www.lsac.org/lsat/taking-lsat/test-format/logical-reasoning/logical-reasoning-sample-questions (last visited July 2, 2020).

for website ads. We concluded that consumer response to the print ads was probably below par as well.

The executive's reasoning does which one of the following?

a. bases an educated prediction of the intensity of a phenomenon on information about the intensity of that phenomenon's cause

b. uses information about the typical frequency of events of a general kind to draw a conclusion about the probability of a particular event of that kind

c. infers a statistical generalization from claims about a large number of specific instances

d. uses a case in which direct evidence is available to draw a conclusion about an analogous case in which direct evidence is unavailable

e. bases a prediction about future events on facts about recent comparable events

Explanation for Question:

This question asks you to identify how the executive's reasoning proceeds. The ads discussed by the executive appeared in two places—in a magazine and on the magazine's website. Some information is available concerning the effect of the website ads on consumers, but no consumer response information is available about the print ads. The executive's remarks suggest that the ads that appeared in print and on the website were basically the same, or very similar. The executive reasoned that information about the effect of the website ads could be used as evidence for an inference about how the print ads likely performed. The executive thus used the analogy between the print ads and the website ads to infer something about the print ads. (D), therefore, is the correct response.

Response (A) is incorrect. The executive's conclusion about the likely consumer response to the print ads does not constitute a prediction, but rather a judgment about the events that have already transpired. The executive's conclusion is not based on any reasoning about the cause of the consumer response to the print ads.

Response (B) is incorrect. The executive does conclude that certain events are likely to have transpired on the basis of what was known to have transpired in a similar case, but no distinction can be made in the executive's argument between events of a general kind and a particular event of that kind. There are two types of events in play in the executive's argument and they are of the same level of generality—the response to the website ads and the response to the print ads.

Response (C) is incorrect. The executive does not infer a statistical generalization, which would involve generalizing about a population on the basis of a statistical sample. The executive merely draws a conclusion about the likely occurrence of specific events.

Response (E) is also incorrect. The executive does use the comparability of the print and website ads as the basis for the conclusion drawn; however, as noted above, the executive's conclusion about the likely consumer response to the print ads does not constitute a prediction about future events, but rather a judgment about events that have already transpired.

This was considered **easy** based on the number of test takers who answered it correctly when it appeared on the LSAT.

Writing Sample Section:

There are different opinions regarding whether test takers should include preparing for the writing sample into their study schedule. The best way to answer this is to use your best judgement. I would advise that if you choose not to include it into preparation, at the very least be sure to view an example so that the first time you see a writing sample question is not on the LSAT itself.

For the writing sample, you are not given a score because there is no correct answer since an argument can be made for either choice. You will be presented with 2 choices for the scenario. It is best to formulate your essay with consideration of both choices (in conjunction with the facts provided) and then argue for one choice over the other.

Below is a Writing Sample Example: [5]

BLZ Stores, an established men's clothing retailer with a chain of stores in a major metropolitan area, is selecting a plan for expansion. Using the facts below, write an essay in which you argue for one of the following plans over the other based on the following two criteria:

- The company wants to increase its profits.

---

[5] Law School Admissions Council, Writing Sample Topic, https://www.lsac.org/lsat/lsat-prep/practice-test/writing-sample-topic (last visited July 2, 2020).

- The company wants to ensure its long-term financial stability.

The "national plan" is to open a large number of men's clothing stores throughout the country over a short period of time. In doing this, the company would incur considerable debt. It would also have to greatly increase staff and develop national marketing and distribution capabilities. Many regional companies that adopted this strategy increased their profits dramatically. A greater number tried and failed, suffering severe financial consequences. BLZ is not well known outside its home area. Research indicates that the BLZ name is viewed positively by those who know it. National clothing chains can offer lower prices because of their greater buying power. BLZ currently faces increasingly heavy competition in its home region from such chains.

The "regional plan" is to increase the number and size of stores in the company's home region and upgrade their facilities, product quality, and service. This could be achieved for the most part with existing cash reserves. These upgrades would generally increase the prices that BLZ charges. In one trial store in which such changes were implemented, sales and profits have increased. The local population is growing. BLZ enjoys strong customer loyalty. Regional expansion could be accomplished primarily using BLZ's experienced and loyal staff and would allow continued reliance on known and trusted suppliers, contractors, and other business connections.

> **No explanation will be provided either answer choice is acceptable depending on the facts presented with it.**

Now that we have covered all sections of the LSAT, it is up to you to hone in on your individual skills, hold yourself accountable and give it all you've got!

Remember: Be consistent in your studying. Don't let your 3 a.m. brain get the best of you, this will be a challenge to some degree for many but continue to focus on your 3 "why's."

Take mental breaks when needed but don't quit.

Do the best you can with what you have. Focus on getting the highest score that you can. Take the LSAT with confidence and own it!

LSAT FLEX

LSAT-FLEX is a newly introduced method of taking the LSAT in light of the recent COVID-19 Pandemic. There are differences compared to the traditional LSAT but many similarities as well. [6]

Two Major Differences are:

1) The test is done remotely instead of the traditional testing center. This means that LSAT-Flex test takers will need to have a computer, desktop or laptop with Mac or Windows operating system

---

[6] Law School Admissions Council, Introducing LSAT-Flex, https://www.lsac.org/update-coronavirus-and-lsat/lsat-flex (last visited July 5, 2020).

(and a quiet area). The test it will also be proctored (currently through ProctorU)

2) There is only ONE Logic Reasoning (LR) Section and NO unscored section (a total 3 sections) This decreases the overall time of the LSAT and there are NO Breaks given.

3) You get to choose a time that works best for you instead of traditionally having to take the test at the designated time.

The Similarities:

1) The LSAT Flex has the same $200 fee and process for registration.

2) Same items that you are allowed to bring into the exam. You bring the 5 blank pieces of scratch paper versus being given the paper at the testing center. (Number 2 pencil, highlighter, valid id etc.)

3) Same option to cancel scores but it must be done within 6 days.

LSAT Flex Tips:

a. If you are in need to a loaner device to take the LSAT on, reach out the LSAC and ask for assistance, this also includes the waivers that we will speak about in the following chapter.

b. Take practice exams! Power Score has LSAT Flex exams. Do a quick google search of any other prep companies that have tests that are geared towards LSAT-FLEX.

c. If you can't find any, use the traditional tests and take them under the assumption that ALL SECTIONS COUNT. With LSAT-Flex, there's no cushion section. You know that every question you look at is factored into your score. This is how you should study anyway whether it be Flex or standard LSAT.

All in all, I would give the same advice for both exams. Answer all questions to best of your ability. Study hard, efficiently and give yourself enough time to review the foundation of each section and create drills. Treat the LSAT like a Job. Even if that job is virtual.

Clock in. Do the work. This is one thing that is within your control. Seek guidance whenever needed.

CHAPTER 4

Everyone Isn't Harvard Bound

You've taken the LSAT and now you have options: apply to law school with your current score or make the decision to retake the LSAT. If you are considering retaking the LSAT:

1. Evaluate the likelihood of your acceptance into any law school based on your current score.

2. Research the schools that fall within your score range and see what they have to offer.

3. Reevaluate your study plan to see if there is room for improvement (i.e. Did you need more time to study? Did you cover all of the material? etc.)

4. Determine if your target score is realistic.

Of all of the considerations, the last is the most difficult. I know that everyone wants to perform exceptionally well on the LSAT. BUT it is vital to understand that everyone does not get 180. Everyone isn't Harvard bound. Not that these 2 things are synonymous. IT IS OKAY.

This is not to discourage you from attaining either of those if they're your goals but to show that there's nothing wrong with NOT attaining them. Not everyone has the same aspirations.

The decision to retake should not be taken lightly. Use your best judgment and do what's best for you.

If you've decided to apply to law school, I suggest taking full advantage of the second consideration. Compare several law schools, even your dream school. Law school is a huge investment.

Below are thr factors to consider when considering applying to law school:

a. GPA/LSAT Median Score: Does your score fall within the school's range or close to it?

b. Location: are you willing to relocate and have you allocated funds to prepare for that? Do you prefer to stay close to home for support? Do you prefer sunshine over snow?

c. Full time or part time program: Does the school offer an alternative to full time if you plan to work during the school year?

d. Acceptance rate: At what percentage does the law schools accepts students each year?

e. Cost of attendance: How do you plan to pay for your education? Scholarships, loans, out of pocket etc.

f. Diverse Environment: Do you prefer to attend a law school that has more women than men, more minority students? etc.?

g. What you intend to do with your law degree: This is often left out when deciding on a law school.

Most people believe that lawyers generally make 6 figures or more. This is not true for all. Consider if you intend to go into public service, use the degree for career advancement at your current place of employment among other career paths before deciding to commit to a school (especially if you will be paying 6 figures to attend).

Of course, this is not an exclusive list; there are things that you must consider based on your own personal circumstances. However, it provides you with different items to consider making an informed decision that will best benefit you. Knowing that you have evaluated all options will give you peace of mind later. That said, create a list of schools that you would like to apply to in order to increase your options.

So you've decided on a law school, what's next? (yes, more lists)

What you'll need to apply to law school (for a majority of them)

1. Letters of Recommendation

2. Personal Statement

3. Resume

4. Transcripts

5. LSAC account to submit documents

Letters of Recommendations

The number of letters of recommendation required for your application will depend on the law school. Many schools will request that at least one of the recommenders be a previous professor. Establish genuine relationships with your professors and choose one who will give you a strong letter. Having at least 3 letters of recommendations would suffice for most schools.

When considering who will write your letters of recommendation, ask yourself if the person you're requesting knows you well enough to personally recommend you. Now is not the time to have a generic letter. Having someone to speak to your character and your ability to perform is vital.

When you request a letter of recommendation, give your recommender adequate time to complete it. DO NOT ask for a letter a week before you plan on applying. Ideally, giving your recommender 1 month gives you enough time to send the request and find someone else if there is no response or if your recommender is unable to complete the letter for you.

Additionally, when requesting a letter, be sure to personalize the request. The letter will be of no use to you if the recommender doesn't remember who you are.

As part of that personalization, add facts about yourself and how you and the recommender know each other. "I was a student in your x,y,z course and I loved when we covered…"

Next, tell them who you are on a personal level. They will be able to add this information to your letter. For example, tell them why you want to attend law school, if you faced any adversity during school, or if there were times where you "rose to the occasion" (did you work while in school, take care of children etc.), make sure to include that. Also mention that you have received any recognitions and/or awards.

Finally thank them for their consideration both before and after they write the letter.

"Fun" fact: You as the requestor will not see what the recommender has written about you for your LOR. The recommender submits the letter directly to LSAC. This is why it's important to give your recommender all of the information ahead of time and provide them with adequate time to complete it.

You don't want a rushed product instead a well thought out and letter of recommendation.

Be sure to have back up recommenders should someone decline or not be able to make the deadline. Don't take it personally, just move on to the next person. You want someone who truly supports you to give you a letter of recommendation.

Personal Statement

Your personal statement is the opportunity for the admission committee to get to know you as a candidate. Most law schools request a personal statement of 2 pages or shorter with the to complete an optional addendum and/or diversity statement.

It's vital to remember to be yourself when writing your personal statement. Make your first paragraph eye catching and interesting. Put yourself in the admission committee's shoes. They are reviewing multiple statements, some far shorter times than others, you want your letter of recommendation to stand out and engage them to continue reading.

Keep your wording simple; "big" words are not necessary. While having an extensive vocabulary can beneficial, now is not the time to display your new word of the day.

PROOFREAD multiple times and have others read your statement for you too. It also helps to read it aloud after it is written and make necessary edits. You want to put your best foot forward. Your personal statement is an extension of yourself; tell your story correctly.

Some law schools will give you the opportunity to shape your personal statement as you wish while other schools will have a specific topic or question to answer. If the latter is the case, stick to what is being asked of you. Going off on tangents will not work in your favor.

DO NOT use legal jargon because misuse of them is possible and you don't want that. Your personal statement is NOT the time to pretend to be a lawyer.

Be unique. Everyone wants to "save the world" or "help others." These are widely used topics of personal statements. Instead, discuss why you want to go to law school and how your personal experiences have shaped you and the good that you want to do (For example, internships, volunteer event, studying abroad, etc.)

DO NOT use the personal statement to discuss irregularities in your application or to discuss what your resume has already stated. Irregularities is what the addendum is for.

An addendum should be short in length, no more than a page. It should be used to explain any irregularities or what could be perceived as red flags. The goal is not to make excuses or justifications but to explain the situations and why they should not negatively affect your candidacy.

You should consider submitting an addendum if your LSAT and/or GPA is low or you have criminal or disciplinary record or any other extenuating circumstances. If you've made a mistake, show remorse.

Overall, strategically use your addendum to show accountability and explanations. A diversity statement is used to show how you will bring a unique contribution and help diversify the incoming class. This statement is normally based on gender, race, sexual orientation, socioeconomic background and family education etc. This statement should follow a similar structure of addendum in length.

The goal is to have a strong personal statement so that all other statements, like an addendum, do not take away from your application.

Resume

Your resume should be complete, accurate, and professional. Highlight information that makes you stand out as an applicant. If you were on the Dean's List, now is the time to say it. President of an organization? Led a volunteer event for an awesome cause? SAY IT.

Your resume should speak to the things that you've done and if you haven't done anything as of yet, I would advise that you get on it. Perform well in your studies so that you can add that to your resume, choose genuine volunteer opportunities that you enjoy. You will be able to adequately explain the details of your volunteer work involvement. Speaking of details, please note the admissions committee is not a friend who you speak to on a regular basis so refrain from using profanity and text or other informal language.

Check your margins and choose a professional font. Selecting the Times New Roman 12-point font is safe and professional. Have someone review your resume and make the necessary edits. While it's a resume for law school, treat it as a resume for a job because again, you want to put your best foot forward. The last thing that you want is for the admission committee to discount your application because of something as simple as your resume.

Transcripts

You will need to request transcripts from all of the universities that you have attended. From these, the LSAC will create a law school report. This report may calculate your GPA differently than your universities (ex. repeating classes). This report costs $45 each and you will be charged this for each law school that you apply to.

What you need to know most is that you should send all of the transcripts. DO NOT leave out any just because your grades were not the best. Please do not risk being academically dishonest. Most Universities have an online database to submit requests. Use the form that you will receive from your LSAC account to request transcripts.

Now that you know what you need and have everything completed, you have what I like to call your law school application portfolio.

Credential Assembly Service Registration

Depending on the number of law schools you apply to, you will need to pay for the Credential Assembly Service (CAS). The benefit of service is that it makes the application process easier and more streamlined. The current price for this service is $195. You purchase the CAS through your LSAC account. CAS stores all of your necessities for applying to law school. You submit all of your professional documents (Including letters of recommendation, transcripts, law school applications, and LSAT score) and it is sent to all of the law schools that you are applying to.

This is an added cost in addition to the $45 for each law school report that will be sent to the schools. The benefit of having CAS is that it allows you to save both time and money in the long run. You have one location that houses all of your important information. Instead of having transcripts sent to every school, you have them sent to CAS and they are sent out to schools from there. This saves you money and time if you are applying to multiple schools. Majority of law schools require everything be done through CAS instead of having items sent directly to their admission's office.

If application costs are an issue, there are always waivers that you can apply for when applying to law school, including application fee waivers and LSAT waivers, but applying for these waivers should be done as soon as possible so that you can better prepare for the financial costs of applying to law school.

CHAPTER 5

Finding Your Tribe

Law school is a road less traveled for many, so it is important to connect early on with others that are going through the same journey. Doing so allows you to recognize that you are not alone. Connecting with others allows you to find encouragement and support as you reach your goals. It also gives you accountability partners.

You can find many of these tribes on social media. How do you find them? The search bar is your friend. I would suggest utilizing key terms such as: law school, law, esquire, or jd to name a few. This search should garner desired results.

You can also search hashtags that pertain to what you're looking for. #lawschoolbound #lsat.

When all else fails, USE GOOGLE. This will give you a place to start or narrow searches but using the key terms should get you where you need to go. Below you will find two tribes that have become home for me on this journey, in addition to the tribe that I have also created. They have both been extremely resourceful to me and they have been gracious enough to be a part this project and possibly a tribe to you all as well. There are many more out there so don't be afraid to join many groups and learn from each of them. It's perfectly fine to be a part of more than one tribe.

Black Girls Do Law ™

The organization Black Girls Do Law ™ (BGDL) is a great community that is aimed towards empowering, supporting, and promoting black women legal professionals. BGDL's goal is to network, connect, and offer mentorship.

BGDL's founder, Destiny Williams, believed that the legal industry was lacking a specific and safe place for black women in the legal profession. There was an abundance of black lawyer organizations, as well as female/women lawyer spaces, but little to no spaces dedicated specifically for BLACK women in the legal profession.

While some legal organizations only cater to law students and/or attorneys, BGDL welcomes ALL black women in the legal industry - regardless of where you are in your journey. This includes black women who are specifically paralegals, legal assistants, attorneys, judges, law students, law professors, and aspiring law students.

Destiny Williams, Esq. is a North Carolina native. She is currently barred in and resides in North Carolina. She received her bachelor's degree in Criminal Justice from East Carolina University in 2011 and her Juris Doctor from Howard University School of Law in 2017. When she clocks out from her legal duties and BGDL, she enjoys time with her husband, Zerell, and their son, Julian.

The Law School Mentor

Yoshi Haynie (@yoshihaynie) is the founder of @TheLawSchoolMentor, found on Instagram and Facebook. He recently graduated with honors and top 7% from the UIC John Marshall Law School in Chicago. In law school, Yoshi served as the Student Bar Association President his 3L year, he also participated in The John Marshall Law Review, Moot Court Honors Council, served on the executive board of multiple executive student organizations, and made the Dean's List every semester. He CALI'd (received the highest grade) in 2 classes and volunteered with multiple bar associations throughout law school.

Outside of law school he manages two brands: @thelawschoolmentor (a platform to help current and prospective law students thrive in law school) and @encourageu2 (a non-profit with a social media initiative to spread positivity, motivate, inspire, and encourage others in a world where it can be hard to remain hopeful, especially with the landscape of social media). Yoshi is a firm believer that you can learn from anyone, you just have to be willing to listen.

Yoshi started The Law School Mentor for a number of different reasons. He found himself mentoring students and finding a passion to share his experience and resources with others, especially diverse students. He realized most of us, himself included, were first-generation and had a "I just have to survive law school" mentality, which was thought to bring success. But he wanted to change that. He realized that with diversity initiatives and the right mentality, we could not just survive, but really thrive. So, he wanted to change the survival mentality to encourage others to exceed expectations and reach for their wildest dreams, as well as using his platform, access, and knowledge to propel those who come behind him into the highest achievement.

Secondly, Yoshi wanted to be a positive representation of what was possible. He was told so many times he would never see inside the walls of a big law firm without going to a Top15 or Top 20 school. He adopted the mentality that all he needed was a chance, a foot in the door, and he would do the rest. So, he excelled in grades, built hundreds of relationships, and obtained an offer from Kirkland & Ellis, LLP as a transactional corporate associate.

Given all of that, he wanted to share his story to as many people to give them hope and inspiration, and really a wealth of resources that he's accumulated to encourage, motivate, and inspire the generation after him to achieve their wildest dreams.

The Juris Society ™

I created The Juris Society (@thejurissociety_ on Instagram) because I noticed a lack of information in the marketplace that catered to the direct needs of first-generation aspiring law students. It is lonely navigating a road less traveled, especially for minorities. I decided to establish a community where first-generation aspiring law students could come to be encouraged, empowered, and equipped to be admitted into law school.

The Juris Society™ was established as a pre-law society where first-generation aspiring law students are given avenues for success. This is done through mentorship (both undergraduate and graduate) as well as Law School Admission Test Prep including administering practice exams, determining the best method of study, study schedule creation, and progress sessions to track mentee's study habits. Application Assistance services are also offered, which include law school application portfolio review of resumes, personal statements, addendum review, diversity statement review, letters of recommendation edits, letters of continued interest review, and so much more. Mentees also learn professional etiquette, techniques to combat their "3 a.m. Brain" and to trust their abilities. The Juris Society™ Mantra is "Transparency, Tenacity & Triumph."

Mentees are taught to hold themselves and others accountable, to not just simply survive but THRIVE. Additionally, that THEY BELONG IN THE ROOM. They are affirmed that they are valuable trailblazers and they contribute to the overall diversity of the legal field.

The Juris Society provides aid via scholarships to first generation students as a means to combat financial hardship for those in need.

Here, I assist in creating law legacies and the futures of tomorrow.

> "Tell us what brought you to law, we'll help you get there"- **Carletta S.**

A part of finding a tribe is finding a mentor that can assist you along the journey. Mentors have gone where you are trying to go, and they can share information to you that will alleviate you from making mistakes that they made.

How do you market yourself as an ideal mentee? By being a genuine person. Mentor/mentee relationships should happen organically. You don't want to be miserable while speaking with someone and you need to be able to trust them with your struggles, thoughts and trust the advice that they give. They want to trust that you aren't wasting their time and that you value the information that they are giving you. Mentor/Mentee is a give/give relationship. Next, is by being coachable. Your will to succeed must be stronger that your need to hold on to your ego. Understand that while you may have been an expert in a previous subject, law is a foreign topic to you.

You don't want to get a reputation as a know-it-all.

All in all, finding a supportive tribe and a mentor makes all the difference on this journey. Going to law school is about more than just the law. Creating lasting connections will allow you to networking opportunities that sometimes can get you into doors that you may not have been invited to enter otherwise.

Your reputation starts now. Ask yourself, when people hear/see my name, what do I want them to think of?

What is your personal brand? Are you likeable? This may seem a minor point, but it's extremely important because connecting and networking and getting people to offer guidance to you is less likely to happen if they simply do not like you.

These are small things that you will learn as you go on the journey, but the purpose of this chapter is to introduce you to resources that have helped me, and others, along the way.

There are things that never go out of style, such as being a good human, being consistent and reliable, and being courteous to everyone that you meet.

And if you lose your way, always go back to your 3 questions.

1) Why do you want to be an attorney?

2) Why is the goal of "becoming Esquire" important to you?

3) How will this degree and license impact your life as well as others?

Let these questions be your guide. Go back to Chapter 1 whenever you need reassurance.

You get to rest, but you don't get to quit.

You're just getting started.

A Note About The Author

Carletta Sanders is a Mississippi native. She is a first-generation graduate. Carletta received her Bachelor of Science with honors from Park University, Mo in 2019. She is currently a dual J.D./MBA student at Northern Illinois University where she is currently functioning as the President of the Business Law Society, Black Law Students Association in addition to being the founder of The Juris Society™.

Prior to law school, Carletta served in the United States Air Force for 8 years. She has lived all over the globe which attributes to her leadership ability to effectively communicate with others in a variety of settings. She's no stranger to hard work, discipline, and mentorship.

She comes with years of supervisory experience and has been awarded numerous military achievements and recognition.

A Note About The Author

Carletta is available
on all social media platforms.

INSTAGRAM:
@Becomingcarletta.esq,
@thejurissociety_

WEBSITE:
www.thejurissociety.com

TWITTER:
@thejurissociety

FACEBOOK:
The Juris Society

www.ingramcontent.com/pod-product-compliance
Lightning Source LLC
Chambersburg PA
CBHW021913180426
43198CB00034B/404